Understanding Theology

as taught by

Dr. Bruce Ware

BiblicalTraining.org
Because Your Spiritual Growth Matters

Understanding Theology

Student's Guide © Copyrighted 2021 BiblicalTraining.org. All Rights Reserved.

Course content and outline Copyrighted 2021 Dr. Bruce Ware. All Rights Reserved.

Requests for information should be addressed to:

BiblicalTraining.org
523 NE Everett St
Camas WA 98607

ISBN: 9781543273779

All Scripture quotations, unless otherwise indicated, are taken from the Holy Bible, New International Version®, NIV®. Copyright ©1973, 1978, 1984, 2011 by Biblica, Inc.™ Used by permission of Zondervan. All rights reserved worldwide. www.zondervan.com The "NIV" and "New International Version" are trademarks registered in the United States Patent and Trademark Office by Biblica, Inc.™

All rights reserved. No part of this publication may be reproduced, stored in a retrieval system, or transmitted in any form or by any means—electronic, mechanical, photocopy, recording, or any other—except for brief quotations in printed reviews, without the prior permission of BiblicalTraining.org.

Printed in the United States of America

https://www.biblicaltraining.org/understanding-theology/bruce-ware

Table of Contents

BiblicalTraining.org vii
Overview vi
Your Speaker v
Weekly schedule viii
Facilitator's Guide ix

1. Introduction to Theology; Revelation and Scripture . . 3
2. Attributes of God 0
3. The Trinity 15
4. Humanity and Sin 0
5. Person of Christ 7
6. Work of Christ 4
7. The Holy Spirit 38
8. Salvation 42
9. The Church 8
10. Last Things 53

BiblicalTraining.org

BiblicalTraining.org is not-for-profit ministry that gives all people access to a world-class Christian education at no cost. Our classes range from new believers to biblical literacy ("Foundations"), deeper Bible study ("Academy"), and seminary-level training ("Institute").

We are a 501(c)3 not-for-profit and rely solely on the donations of our users. All donations are tax deductible according to the current US tax codes.

DISTINCTIVES

World class. All Bible classes are taught by world-class professors from major seminaries.

Holistic. We want to see students move through content to deep reflection and application.

Configurable. Ministries can use BT lectures as well as their own to design their educational program.

Accessible. BiblicalTraining is a web-based ministry whose content is provided at no cost.

Community-based. We encourage people to learn together, in mentor/apprentice relationships.

Broadly evangelical. Our materials are broadly evangelical, governed by our Statement of Faith, and are not tied to any one church, denomination or tradition.

Partners. We provide the content and delivery mechanisms, and our partner organizations provide the community and mentoring.

Overview

Title: Understanding Theology

Speaker: Dr. Bruce Ware

GOALS

1. Learn the basics of biblical theology
2. Challenge yourself to see what you believe
3. Use theology to pusue spireitual growth

REQUIREMENTS

1. 10 sessions
2. Three hours per session (lesson and discussion)

PREREQUISITES

None

FORMAT

Audio and syncxed slides

Your Speaker

Dr. Bruce Ware is the T. Rupert and Lucille Coleman Professor of Christian Theology (1998). Dr. Ware is a highly esteemed theologian and author in the evangelical world. He came to Southern Seminary from Trinity Evangelical Divinity School where he served as chairman of the Department of Biblical and Systematic Theology. Prior to this, he taught at Western Conservative Baptist Seminary and Bethel Theological Seminary.

EDUCATION

Ph.D., Fuller Theological Seminary

M.A., University of Washington

M.Div., Th.M., Western Conservative Baptist Seminary

B.A., Whitworth College

Cert, Capernwray Bible School

A.S., Judson Baptist College

MAJOR PUBLICATIONS

Ware has written numerous journal articles, book chapters, and book reviews and, along with Thomas Schreiner, co-edited *Still Sovereign*. He also has authored *God's Lesser Glory: The Diminished God of Open Theism*; *God's Greater Glory: The Exalted God of Scripture and the Christian Faith*; *Father, Son, and Holy Spirit: Relationships, Roles, and Relevance*; *Big Truths for Young Hearts: Teaching and Learning the Greatness of God*; and *The Man Christ Jesus: Theological Reflections on the Humanity of Christ*.

Weekly schedule

Listen or watch the lesson. The lesson for each chapter is designed to be listened to outside of your meeting. Each lesson lasts for an hour. This is a crucial step. If the meeting time with your fellow students is going to be productive and encouraging, everyone in the group needs to have listened to and wrestled with the lesson.

Take notes. This guide has the outline for each lesson with a summary of the teaching for each major point. If you are unable to take notes while listening to the lesson, please work through the guide at some point before your meeting.

Questions. Each chapter closes with a series of questions. Some of the questions are data based, confirming that you understand the information. Other questions are more reflective, helping you move beyond the important accumulation of knowledge to challenging you to think through what you are learning about God, yourself and others, and finally to application. Our encouragement is to think through your answers before your meeting and then use the meeting to share your thoughts and interact with others.

MEETING TOGETHER

While some people may have to study on their own, we strongly recommend finding a group with which you can study.

A group provides encouragement to finish the class.

Interacting with others, their understanding and insight, is the most effective way to sharpen your own thoughts and beliefs.

Just as you will need the help of others from time to time, so also they will need your help.

Facilitator's Guide

If you are leading the group or mentoring an individual, here are some suggestions that should help you.

Your role is to facilitate. This is not an opportunity for you to teach. In fact, the less visible role you take, the better. Your role is to listen and bring out the best in the other people.

Preparation. Be sure to have done your homework thoroughly. Have listened to the lesson and think carefully through the questions. Have an answer for each question that will get the conversation going. A great question is, "What is the Lord teaching you this week?"

Creativity. What works to help one person understand may not help another. So listen to the conversation and pray that the Lord help you bring out the greatest interaction among all the people.

Correct error. This is difficult. If someone says something that isn't right, you don't want to come down on them, telling them they are wrong and shutting down their participation. On the other hand, if you let an obvious error pass, the rest of the group may think you agree and what was said was correct. So look for gracious ways to suggest that perhaps the person's comment was incorrect.

Focus. Stay focused on Jesus and the Bible, not on church or religious traditions.

Lead the discussion. People don't want to listen to a sharing of common ignorance. Lead by asking questions that will prompt others to think.

Silence. Don't be afraid of silence. It may mean nothing more than people are thinking. But if the conversation lags, then ask thought-provoking questions to get the discussion started, and then step out of the way.

Discipleship. Be acutely aware of how you can mentor the people in the group. Meet with them for coffee. Share some life with them. Jesus' Great Commission is to teach people to obey, and the only way this happens is in relationship.

Different perspectives. People process information and express themselves in different ways based on their background, previous experience, culture, religion and other factors. Encourage an atmosphere that allows people to share honestly and respectfully.

Privacy. All discussions are private, not to be shared outside the group unless otherwise specified.

Goal. The goal of this study is not just increased knowledge; it is transformation. Don't be content with people getting the "right" answers. The Pharisees got the "right" answer, and many of them never made it to heaven (Matt 5:20).

Relationships. Share everyone's name, email and phone number so people can communicate during the week and follow up on prayer requests. You may want to set up a way to share throughout the week using Slack or WhatsApp.

Finish well. Encourage the people to make the necessary commitment to do the work, think reflectively over the questions, and complete the class.

Prayer. Begin and end every meeting with prayer. Please don't do the quick "one-prayer-covers-all" approach. Manage the time so all of you can pray over what you have learned and with what you have been challenged. Pray regularly for each individual in the meeting.

1

Introduction to Theology; Revelation and Scripture

I. WHAT IS EVANGELICAL SYSTEMATIC THEOLOGY

A. Definition

Study and organization of what can be known about God from Scripture

B. Elaboration on the definition

1. The subject matter

God and his relation to the created universe

2. The sources

Scripture is the primary source

3. The structure

Comprehensive study and coherent organization

4. The setting

Understandable and applicable to contemporary audiences

5. The satisfaction

   The purpose of systematic theology is that you are strengthened and satisfied in God

II. **WHY STUDY EVANGELICAL THEOLOGY**

   A. **Comprehensive Scriptural vantage point**

   Looking at all of the teaching of the Bible on various subjects

   B. **Interpretive guide**

   Guideline for interpreting passages of Scripture

C. **Religious pluralism**

   Systematic Theology can give you confidence in what you believe and how to articulate it

D. **Head, heart, hands, habitat**

   Understanding the truth, allowing truth to change you and then living differently as a result

III. **REVELATION**

   A. **The concept of revelation**

   The act of God by which he uncovers who he is

B. Forms of revelation

   1. General revelation

      Information about God that everyone can see

   1. Special revelation

      Specific revelatory acts where God makes himself known to certain people

IV. INSPIRATION OF SCRIPTURE

   A. Definition

      God inspired people to write the Scriptures

B. Key Passages

2 Timothy 3:16-17, 2 Peter 1:20-21, 1 Corinthians 2:13

V. INERRANCY OF SCRIPTURE

A. What is the issue?

It is reasonable to trust the Bible

B. Defining inerrancy

All that the Scripture teaches or intends to present as truth is true

C. Authority and inerrancy

Only an inspired, inerrant Bible is fully authoritative for your life, your faith and your practice

REFLECTION QUESTIONS

1. What does systematic theology have to do with your own relationship with God? Do you think that understanding theology helps people have a better relationship with God? Why or why not?

2. Read Psalm 34:8. What does this verse have to do with studying systematic theology? How can it help you appreciate what theology is all about?

3. What does systematic theology have to do with what we actually do in church?

4. What are some questions you have about theology that you would like to learn more about as a result of this study? Why are those questions important to you?

5. What are your basic goals for this study? What do you need to do to make sure that you accomplish those goals during this study?

6. Have you ever had an experience where you felt that you had learned something about God from creation? What was that like? What did you learn?

7. How is learning about God through creation different from learning about God from the Bible? Why are both of these important? How can you make sure that you are including both avenues of revelation in your own life?

8. Read and reflect on 2 Timothy 3:16. In what ways have you found the Bible to be 'profitable' in your own life? Have you ever found the Bible (or parts of the Bible) to be unprofitable? Why do you think that was? What are some things you might be able to do to remedy that?

9. Why is it important to affirm the inerrancy of the Bible? How can understanding increase your confidence in the Bible? How should it affect the way that we approach the Bible?

2

Attributes of God

I. **INTRODUCTION**

   A. **Need to know God**

   "What comes into our minds when we think about God is the most important thing about us." (A. W. Tozer)

B. Classification of Attributes

1. Incommunicable

Attributes that are true of God alone

2. Transcendent vs. immanent

God exists apart from creation and also in relationship with humans

C. Need for methodological balance in the doctrine of God

It's important to acknowledge each attribute of God without diminishing others

II. INCOMMUNICABLE ATTRIBUTES

A. Self-existence

It is the nature of God to exist

B. Self-sufficiency

God possesses within himself all that is required for being God

C. Infinity

There are no boundaries, limitations or restrictions on God's qualities

D. Omnipresence

God is not limited in his existence by space

E. Eternity

God is not limited in his existence by time

F. Immutability

God cannot change in his attributes

III. COMMUNICABLE ATTRIBUTES

A. Intellectual attributes

1. Omniscience

God knows all that is knowable

2. Omnisapience

God is all-wise

B. Moral Attributes

1. Goodness

God shows kindness to others

2. Holiness

God is eternally separate and distinct from all impurity

C. Attributes of God's rulership

1. Omnipotence

God is able to perform anything consistent with his nature as God

2. Sovereignty

God plans and carries out his perfect will

REFLECTION QUESTIONS

1. What do you think A. W. Tozer meant when he said that what we think about God is the most important thing about us? What does your image of God say about you? Where does it need to change?

2. Which of the attributes covered in this study is hardest for you to understand? What can you do to increase your understanding of God in that area?

3. How can attributes like self-existence, self-sufficiency, and omnipresence be a source of encouragement and comfort for believers? What can you do this week to develop a continual awareness of God's presence?

4. Why is it important to affirm God's omnipotence and sovereignty? How should this be a source of comfort to believers? Why do you think some people might not like these attributes? How can you help them appreciate these attributes more?

3

The Trinity

I. **SCRIPTURAL MONOTHEISM**

   A. Old Testament Perspectives on God's Oneness

   Both the Pentateuch and the prophets instruct people to worship God alone

   B. New Testament Perspectives on God's Oneness

   Both Jesus and the letters of the New Testament affirm that people should worship the only true God

II. SCRIPTURAL TRINITARIANISM

A. Scriptural affirmations of the triune God

God the Father, Jesus and the Holy Spirit are affirmed as God throughout the New Testament

B. A brief history of the doctrine of the Trinity

1. Christological background

The nature of Jesus is a central question in understanding the Trinity

2. Monarchian heresies

This belief describes God the Father as the monarch over all, from whom everything comes.

3. The church's rejection of monarchianism

The Nicene creed states that the essence of the Son is identical to the essence of the Father

4. Augustine on the Trinity

The Trinity is unique and there is not an analogy that can completely explain it

C. The immanent and economic Trinities

1. The immanent Trinity

The affirmation the reality of one God; Father, Son and Spirit who exists as God apart from creation

2. **The economic Trinity**

   There is equality of essence and an authority/submission relationship

REFLECTION QUESTIONS

1. What difference does the doctrine of the Trinity make for how we live, worship, and do ministry? In other words, do you think it has significance for everyday life?

2. Why do you think the early church reacted so strongly to different ideas about the Trinity (e.g. modalism)? Why did they think the doctrine of the Trinity was so important?

3. How important is the doctrine of the Trinity in your spiritual life? What is one thing that you can do this week to make the doctrine of the Trinity more important to you?

4. Most Christians believe that the doctrine of the Trinity is ultimately a 'mystery' (that is, we'll never really understand how God can be both one and three). How can thinking about the 'mystery' of God help us worship Him more deeply?

4

Humanity and Sin

I. **HUMANITY'S ORIGIN: GOD THE CREATOR OF HUMAN BEINGS**

   A. **There is a special place for the formation of humanity**

   The terms that are used to describe the formation of the man and the woman indicate design, purpose and intent

   B. **A brief theology of humanity's creation by God**

   Humans were created by God with moral freedom and responsibility

II. HUMANITY'S CONSTITUTION

A. Theories of the structure of human nature

1. Monism

Body and soul are combined so you can't distinguish between them

2. Dichotomy

Humans are made up of material and immaterial, body and soul

3. Trichotomy

Humans are made up of body, soul and spirit

B. Transmission of the soul

1. Creationism

God creates each soul and joins it with a human body

2. Traducianism

The process of reproduction produces humans with bodies and souls

III. IMAGE OF GOD

A. Major understandings of the, "image of God"

1. Structural understanding

The essence of our makeup as humans reflects the image of God

2. Relational understanding

The male-female relationship reflects the image of God

3. Functional understanding

We are called to do what God has commanded us to do

B. The image of God, the Fall, and its renewal

1. Ancient Near-Eastern background

The image of God was concept that was used prominently in the cultures of the ancient Near-East

2. **Image of God: structural, relational and functional**

   It is reflected in the humans were created and how they were meant to function

3. **Effects of the fall and our restoration into the image of Christ**

   The Fall distorted the image of God in humans and Christ provides a way to restore it

IV. NATURE OF SIN

A. Essence of sin

1. **Urge for independence from God**

   Humans want to be the ultimate authority in their own lives

2. Three kinds of urges for independence

Hedonistic, covetous and prideful

B. Total depravity

Every part of human nature is affected by sin

C. Total inability

Humans are not able on their own to make choices that are pleasing to God

D. Acts of personal sin

In both outward actions and inward attitudes, all humans commit sinful acts and also fail to do what they ought to do

E. Systemic or social manifestations of sin

Good structures are used for evil and structures are formed for the purpose of doing evil

V. ORIGINAL SIN

A. Definition

The sin nature is passed on to each person

B. Theories of original sin

1. Federal or representative theory

When Adam sinned, he brought sin on the whole human race

2. Realist or Augustinian theory

The sin of Adam and Eve is passed on through reproduction

REFLECTION QUESTIONS

1. Read Genesis 1:26-28. How does it make you feel to realize that you are made in the image of God? Who is someone in your life that you have a difficult time seeing this way? How can you begin seeing them as one of God's image-bearers?

2. Can you see any tendencies toward "independence from God" in your own life? What can you do this week to increase your dependence on God in this area? Of the three kinds of sinful independence discussed, which seems most difficult for you?

3. Why is "total depravity" important for us to understand? Why do you think some people would have a hard time with this doctrine? How can you help them understand and appreciate it more?

4. Can you think of any areas in which Christians tend to be less concerned about inward attitudes than they are about external actions? What do you think about that? Do you see any signs of that in your own life?

5. Can you think of any examples of "evil structures" or "social manifestations of sin" in your city? What responsibility do you think that Christians and Christian churches have for addressing these evil social structures? What responsibility do you have?

5

Person of Christ

I. CHRIST'S PRE-INCARNATE EXISTENCE

   A. Jesus as the "Lord" of the Old Testament

      Isaiah 6:3; 7:14; 9:6-7; 40:3

   B. The testimony of Jesus about his own pre-existence

      John 8:58; 17:5

II. INCARNATION

A. Jesus as prophet

Jesus came to earth as the ultimate prophet. Hebrews describes him as being superior to Moses

B. Jesus as priest

Jesus fulfills the role of high priest and is eternal

C. Jesus as king

Jesus fulfilled the Davidic covenant

III. **DEITY OF CHRIST**

   A. The names of God are applied to Christ

   Some examples are, "God," "Son of God," and "Son of Man"

   B. The attributes of God alone are applied to Christ

   Eternal existence and immutability

   C. The works that only God does are done by Christ

   Creation, forgiving sins and giving eternal life

D. The worship belonging to God alone is given to Christ

The magi came to worship him soon after he was born, people worshipped him during his ministry on earth and he will be worshipped at the end of the age

E. Jesus claims to be God

His statements are clear enough that some people wanted to stone him for blasphemy

IV. HUMANITY OF CHRIST

A. The Old Testament teaches that the Messiah who would come would be human

Isaiah 7:14; Micah 5:30

B. Christ's own life indicates his humanity

He was born, he developed physically and he experienced and expressed emotions

C. Christ remains human forever

When Christ comes again at the end of the age, he will return in bodily form

V. THE EMPTYING (KENOSIS) OF CHRIST: PHILIPPIANS 2:6-8

A. Key terms

Form (*morphe*), equality (*isos*), he emptied himself (*ekenosin*)

B. The Meaning of Kenosis

Emptying by adding

VI. THE SINLESSNESS (IMPECCABILITY) OF CHRIST

A. The meaning of the term, "impeccability"

It was impossible for Christ to sin

B. Support for impeccability

The temptations that Christ faced were real but he did not sin and could not sin

VII. HYPOSTATIC UNION AND THE COUNCIL OF CHALCEDON IN A.D. 451

A. Erroneous views of Christ prior to Chalcedon

Apollinarian view and Nestorian view

B. Orthodox decision

Christ was a unified person with two natures

REFLECTION QUESTIONS

1. Reflect for a while on Christ's three roles of Prophet, Priest, and King. What does each reveal about who Jesus was and what he came to do? How can each be a source of comfort and an encouragement to worship?

2. Why did the early church think it was so important to emphasize both the full deity and fully humanity of Jesus? Why is it important for us to continue to emphasize both of these truths today?

3. Read Philippians 2:1-11. What "attitude" did Paul want us to see in Jesus and model in our own lives? Are there any areas of your life in which you are not modeling this attitude? What needs to change?

4. Why is it important to recognize both that Jesus never sinned and that he was tempted just like we are? How can this encourage us to greater faithfulness?

6

Work of Christ

I. **PAST WORK: CHRIST, THE ATONING SAVIOR**

   A. **Aspects of the atonement**

      1. **Sacrifice**

         Animal sacrifices looked forward to Christ's death which was the ultimate sacrifice

2. Substitution

The Old Testament prophesied and the New Testament affirms that there is one who died as a substitute for your sin

3. Redemption

God paid the price necessary to deliver you from sin

4. Propitiation

The satisfaction of God's judgment against our sin

5. Expiation

Your responsibility to pay the penalty for your sin has been removed by Christ

6. Reconciliation

The change of relationship between you and God in which alienation and enmity are replaced by peace and acceptance

B. Atonement and the resurrection

The resurrection declares that the penalty for sin has been paid and the power of sin is defeated

II. PRESENT WORK: CHRIST AS MEDIATOR AND LORD

A. Mediator

Christ pleads our case before the Father

B. Lord

Christ is the head of the body of the church

III. FUTURE WORK: CHRIST AS COMING JUDGE AND REIGNING KING

A. Coming judge

When Christ returns at the end of the age, he will require everyone to give an account

B. Reigning king

Christ will establish his throne and reign over earth

REFLECTION QUESTIONS

1. Read and reflect on Isaiah 53. What does this reveal to you about the nature of Christ's work on the cross? If you can, meditate and pray over portions of this chapter every day this week.

2. Why is "redemption" such an important aspect of the atonement? Reflect for a while on your own life. What has Christ redeemed you from? What has he redeemed you for? How can you share your story of redemption with someone this week?

3. Why might people in our society struggle to understand propitiation as an aspect of the atonement? Why is it important? How can you help them understand and appreciate it more?

4. Read Hebrews 7:23-28. How does this passage help you appreciate Christ's continual role as our mediator? Why is this important to understand?

7

The Holy Spirit

I. **PERSON OF THE HOLY SPIRIT**

   A. **Personhood of the Holy Spirit**

   1. **The Holy Spirit has the attributes of a person**

      The Holy Spirit is described as having intellect, emotion and will

2. The Holy Spirit performs the actions of a person

The Holy Spirit teaches, leads and bears witness

3. The Holy Spirit is treated as a person

The Holy Spirit can be resisted, grieved, insulted, lied to and blasphemed

4. Personal pronouns are used to refer to the Holy Spirit

In some places in the New Testament, the Holy Spirit is referred to by using a demonstrative pronoun in the masculine case

B. Deity of the Holy Spirit

1. The Holy Spirit is declared to be God

Prophetic quotes from God are attributed to the Holy Spirit

2. The Holy Spirits shares unique attributes of God

Eternal existence, omniscience, omnipotence

3. The Holy Spirit does works that are unique to God

Creation, regeneration, sanctification, resurrection

4. The Holy Spirit has prerogatives of deity

The Spirit sends out missionaries and guides people in their ministries

5. Triadic passages

There are passages that speak of the Father, Son and Holy Spirt

II. WORK OF THE HOLY SPIRIT

A. Work of the Holy Spirit in the Old Testament

1. Old Testament references

References to the Spirit of God

2. Empowerment

The Holy Spirit empowers people for specific ministries or tasks

3. Prophetic visions about the future role of the Holy Spirit

    What the Holy Spirit will do in the latter days

B. The Holy Spirit in the life and ministry of Jesus

  1. Expectation of the Spirit-empowered Messiah

      Isaiah 11:1-9; 42:1-9; 61:1-3

  2. The Holy Spirit in the life and ministry of Jesus

      Matthew 12:22-32; Acts 10:38

  3. Jesus and the future coming of the Holy Spirit

      John 7:39; 16:7; Acts 2:33

C. The Holy Spirit and the church

1. Pentecost

The empowering of believers by the Holy Spirit

2. Empowerment for witness in the world

Believers spread the message of Christ throughout the world

3. Empowerment for service in the church

The Holy Spirit empowers believers to live together in a way that benefits the community of faith

REFLECTION QUESTIONS

1. Do you think that it is important for Christians to understand that the Holy Spirit is a "person"? Why or why not? What difference might it make for how you relate to the Spirit?

2. Do you think that it is important for Christians to understand that the Holy Spirit is fully divine? Why or why not? What difference might it make for Christian life and ministry?

3. Both the Old and New Testaments emphasize that the Spirit empowers God's people to accomplish the tasks that God has given them. How can this be a source of encouragement to you in your own Christian life? Has God given you any tasks that seem beyond your ability? How can this be a source of encouragement to you with regard to those tasks?

4. Read 1 Corinthians 12. How has the Spirit gifted you to be a blessing to those around you? What can you do this week to use your gifts more effectively to serve others? God has also placed gifted people in your life to bless you. What can you do this week to allow yourself to be blessed by these people?

8

Salvation

I. **ELECTION**

   A. **Scriptural teaching**

   1. **Election in the Old Testament**

      Deuteronomy 7:7; Isaiah 44:1-2

   2. **Election in the New Testament**

      Acts 13:48; Ephesians 1:3-5; Colossians 3:12; 2 Timothy 2:10; 1 Peter 1:1-2

B. Arminian approach: Conditional election

God knows ahead of time who will respond in faith to him and be saved

C. The Calvinist approach: Unconditional election

God elects people unconditionally without taking into account any qualities or actions of individuals

II. CALLING

A. General call

God's proclamation of the gospel through a gospel message to any and all individuals

B. Special or effectual call

A call that ultimately brings a person to saving faith in Christ

III. REGENERATION

A. The nature of regeneration

The giving of life toward God and his renewing work within you by the Holy Spirit

B. The timing of regeneration

The Calvinist view is that regeneration precedes conversion. The Arminian view is that conversion results in regeneration.

Lesson 8 . Salvation

IV. CONVERSION

A. Faith

Saving faith involves your mind, emotions and will in a holistic way

B. Repentance

Turning from sin

V. JUSTIFICATION

A. The method of justification

Initial saving faith resulting in a life characterized by living by faith

B. The results of justification

Being declared not guilty so you can live in the reality of being accepted by God

VI. ADOPTION

A. Nature of adoption

Privileges and responsibilities of being in relationship with God

B. Key verses

Romans 8:15-16; Ephesians 1:5; 2:6-7

VII. SANCTIFICATION

A. Positional sanctification

We are set apart decisively at the moment of saving faith

B. Progressive sanctification

Growth in holiness

VIII. PERSEVERANCE

A. Arminian view

It is possible to reject the salvation you had previously accepted

B. Calvinist view

God sustains those who respond in faith so that they persevere to the end

IX. GLORIFICATION

A. Definition

Complete and final perfection in holiness of the whole person

B. Key verses

Romans 8:23, 29-30; 1 Corinthians 15:35-58; Philippians 3:20-21; 1 Thessalonians 5:23; 1 John 3:2

REFLECTION QUESTIONS

1. Read Ephesians 1:3-14. What are some of the tremendous benefits that flow from being among God's people? Spend some time this week meditating on each of these truths and being encouraged by what it means to be a part of God's elect people.

2. According to 2 Corinthians 5:17, all believers become a "new creature" at salvation (i.e. regeneration). What does this mean? Where do you see this regeneration in your own life? How should this be a source of encouragement to you?

3. What is "justification" and what is the relationship between justification and faith? Why is this important? How would you explain this to someone who does not know anything about the Bible?

4. 4. Read Romans 8:15-16. Spend some time thinking about what it means to be adopted into the family of God. When you pray this week, pray "Abba, Father" and remind yourself of what this means.

5. What things in your life might be hindering your ongoing sanctification (i.e. being made holy for God)? What can you do this week to remove some of those obstacles?

9

The Church

I. **UNIVERSAL CHURCH**

 A. **Nature of the Church**

  1. **Jesus Christ is Lord of the Church**

   Christ moves, directs, governs, leads and rules over his Church

  2. **The Church is formed by the Spirit**

   A community of people who have received and are living in the power of the Spirit

3. The Church unites Jew and gentile

Your identity in the body of Christ does not depend on your ethnicity or nationality

4. The Church is the community of the New Covenant

God calls people to live new lives by the power of the Holy Spirit

5. The Church is a testifying community

The purpose of the Church is to proclaim and exemplify new life in Christ

6. The Church is a worshipping community

Both individual and corporate worship are foundational in the life of the Church

B. New Testament metaphors for the Church

1. Body of Christ

Ephesians 1:20; 4:1-16; 1 Corinthians 12:4-30

2. Bride of Christ

2 Corinthians 11:2; Ephesians 5:25-33; Revelation 19:7-9; 21:9

3. Christ's building

Ephesians 2:19-22; 3:5; 4:11; 1 Peter 2:4-7

4. Christ's flock

John 10:11; Hebrews 13:20; 1 Peter 2:25; 5:4

II. LOCAL CONGREGATIONS

A. Offices in the local church

1. Role of elders

Authority and teaching

2. Role of deacons

Serving in practical ways

3. Roles of men and women in ministry

The egalitarian position is that the Bible teaches that both men and women are able to teach and be in authority in the local church. The complementarian position is that the Bible teaches that only men should teach and be in authority in the local church

B. Organization of the local church

1. Episcopalianism

Bishops have authority over groups of local churches

2. Presbyterianism

Representatives chosen from local churches act as a governing body

3. Congregationalism

Each local church is autonomous

C. Baptism and the Lord's Supper

1. Baptism

Infant baptism and believer's baptism

2. Lord's Supper

Transubstantiation, consubstantiation, the spiritual view and memorial view

REFLECTION QUESTIONS

1. According to Hebrews 10:25, believers should meet together regularly. Why do you think that the author thought this was so important? Do you ever think of going to church as less important, or even optional, for believers? What do you think might contribute to that? What can you do to begin changing that attitude?

2. Read Ephesians 4:1-6. According to this passage, what establishes our unity as believers? Why is this important? How should this affect the way that we view other churches?

3. Read and reflect on Ephesians 5:25-33. What does it mean to say that the church is the Bride of Christ? How does this affect your understanding of the church? How does it make you feel to know that you are a part of that "bride"?

4. Read and reflect on the qualifications for church leaders in 1 Timothy 3:1-13 and 5:17-22. How can this help you appreciate and encourage the leaders in your own church? Take some time this week to pray for the leaders in your church and do something to let them know you appreciate them and their ministry.

10

Last Things

I. **INTRODUCTION**

   A. **The meaning of eschatology**

   Study of what is last

   B. **Value of studying eschatology**

   It motivates and encourages us and gives us hope to endure

II. INTERMEDIATE STATE

A. Unbelievers

Torment and punishment as the await final judgement

B. Believers

Conscious existence in the presence of Christ

III. VIEWS OF THE MILLENIUM

A. Postmillennialism

The second coming of Christ is after the millennium

B. Amillennialism

There is not a millennium in the way that premillennialists describe it

C. Historic premillennialism

Revelation teaches a millennial reign of Christ. The two resurrections indicate a millennial reign

D. Dispensational premillennialism

God will restore Israel to their land and many Jews will come to faith in Christ

IV. VIEWS OF THE TRIBULATION

A. Mid-tribulation rapture

The Church endures the first half of the tribulation but then is taken out of the world by rapture

B. Post-tribulation rapture

Christians will remain on earth during the entire period of the tribulation

C. Pre-tribulation rapture

Christians will be taken out of the world prior to the beginning of the tribulation

V. FINAL JUDGMENT AND THE ETERNAL STATE

A. Final judgment

There is a final judgment for all people and also for believers

B. Hell

Jesus and other writings in the New Testament teach that hell is a real place that is separated from God

C. Heaven

Existence in the presence of God in a physical environment

REFLECTION QUESTIONS

1. Eschatology is often viewed as pointless speculation about the future. This study pointed out seven values we get from studying eschatology. Which of these stands out as most significant for you to appreciate this week? Spend some time meditating on that truth.

2. More important than the timing of the rapture is the importance of being prepared so that we can endure faithfully in the midst of persecution. Read Hebrews 10:32-39. What does this passage have to say about enduring in the face of persecution? How can you be motivated and encouraged by this passage?

3. Romans 8:1 says that there will be "no condemnation" for God's people. But, this study emphasized that there will be a future judgment for God's people. How can these both be true? Why is it important for believers to realize that these are both true? What difference should this make for our life and ministry?

4. Spend a little time this week reading through the passages listed in the study about Heaven. Meditate and pray on these passages, allowing yourself to be encouraged by the hope they express.

If you have any corrections or suggestions about this Student's Guide, please contact support at

www.BiblicalTraining.org/help

We appreciate your feedback.

BiblicalTraining is a non-profit committed to placing world-class teaching in the hands of all people, and therefore our classes can be attended for free. In iorder for us to continue reaching the world and to continue growing, we rely on the donations of our users. Would you consider joining us and making our mission your own? Thank you.

www.biblicaltraining.org/donate

Made in the USA
Monee, IL
31 May 2024